555
Sticker Fun
Dinosaurs

IMAGINE THAT™

Licensed exclusively to Imagine That Publishing Ltd
Tide Mill Way, Woodbridge, Suffolk, IP12 1AP, UK
www.imaginethat.com
Copyright © 2018 Imagine That Group Ltd
EU Authorised Representative, Vulcan Consulting,
38/39 Fitzwilliam Square West, Dublin 2, D02 NX53, Ireland
All rights reserved
18
Manufactured in China

The Triassic Period

The first dinosaurs lived on Earth during the Triassic Period (245-208 million years ago). Fill the Triassic scene with more Eoraptors, one of the earliest-known dinosaurs.

Ambush predators

A group of crafty *Staurikosaurus* lurk in the undergrowth ready to ambush passing lizards. Add these small carnivores to the Triassic scene as they wait for a tasty lizard snack!

No playing on the grass!

There was no grass at the time of the dinosaurs,
so large plant-eating dinosaurs feasted on leaves and ferns.
Add a herd of hungry Mussaurus to this Triassic scene.

Cannibals?

Scientists are finding out new things about dinosaurs all the time. They used to believe that Coelophysis were cannibals, but new evidence disproves this. The hiding lizard had better watch out though!

Triassic seas

Placodus was not a dinosaur, but was a marine reptile that lived in the warm Triassic seas. Add more Placodus to the scene – and some tasty molluscs for them to eat!

The Jurassic Period

It was during the Jurassic Period (208-144 million years ago) that the single area of land on Earth started to crack apart. Add an impressive herd of Stegosaurs to the scene.

Enormous herbivores!

Plant-eating dinosaurs started to get much bigger in the Jurassic period!
Add giant sauropods like Diplodocus, Brachiosaurus and Apatosaurus to
the valley below.

Big carnivores!

Dinosaur predators also got bigger during the Jurassic!
Add fearsome theropods like Allosaurus and Ceratosaurus,
hunting close to the river.

Jurassic seas

The Jurassic seas would not have been a safe place to swim!
They were filled with enormous carnivorous reptiles like Pliosaurus.
Fill the scene with Pliosaurus trying to catch their prey!

Jurassic skies

Pterosaurs were flying reptiles that dominated the skies above the Jurassic landscape. Add a flock of small pterosaurs, called Pterodactyls, flying over the newly formed mountain ranges.

Small but mighty!

Not all dinosaurs in the Jurassic were huge. Small carnivores like the Podokesaurus and Segisaurus thrived! Add some more nimble little hunters to the scene.

The Cretaceous Period

The Cretaceous period (144–65 million years ago) was populated by dinosaurs of all different shapes and sizes. Flowers appeared and there were distinct seasons. Add flowers and plants to complete the scene.

Velociraptors

Velociraptors evolved during the Cretaceous. They were fierce, pack-hunting predators with a large, retractable claw on each foot. Add a hungry, hunting pack to the scene.

Pachycephalosaurus

Pachycephalosaurus challenged rival males to contests to determine superiority. Add the thick-skulled combatants to the scene.

Tyrannosaurus rex

Perhaps the best-known of all dinosaurs, the mighty Tyrannosaurus rex roamed the Cretaceous landscape looking for prey. It had teeth like steak knives! Add a hunting T. rex and a wary herd of Triceratops to the scene.

Ankylosaurus

Not all herbivores would have been easy prey for the large Cretaceous predators. Ankylosaurus were armour-plated and had a large clubbed tail to ward off predators. Add more tank-like dinosaurs to the scene.

Parasaurolophus

The Cretaceous would have been quite noisy! There were lots of earthquakes and active volcanoes and the Parasaurolophus had a hollow crest on their head which they may have used to bellow through. Cover your ears!

Iguanodons

Iguanodons were large herbivores that were able to walk on four or two legs in order to reach vegetation. Huge thumb spikes on each hand were a dangerous weapon against predators. Add a foraging herd to the lush scene.

Spinosaurus

Another fearsome predator during the Cretaceous was the Spinosaurus. It had a remarkable sail on its back and was one of the top predators during this time. Add Spinosaurus to the coastal scene.

Triceratops

Three-horned Triceratops roamed the Cretaceous landscape feeding on plants, much the same as cattle today. They lived in large herds for protection against predators. Make the herd even bigger!

Cretaceous seas

Life in the Cretaceous seas was just as frightening as on the land!
The long-necked Elasmosaurus was one of the main ocean predators.
Add more apex predators and some tasty fish to the scene.

Cretaceous skies

Pterosaurs, or 'winged lizards', reigned supreme in the Cretaceous skies. Quetzalcoatlus was probably the largest flying animal to have ever lived. Add more Quetzalcoatlus and other pterosaurs to the scene.

Extinction

Dinosaurs became extinct about 65 million years ago. Many scientists believe that a giant asteroid hit the Earth. The resulting cloud of poisonous ash would have blocked out the sun and caused the plants, then herbivores and then the carnivores to die out.

Dinosaur world

Not all dinosaurs lived at the same time, but you can use this page to create a scene of all your favourites!